In Level 0, **Book 2** builds o[n]
learnt in Book 1 and focuse[s]
their letters:

s   a   t   p

Special features:

Phonically decodable text
builds reading confidence

Short sentences with
simple language

Is it a tin?

It is Nat.

Repetition of
sounds in
different words

Story Words
Can you match these words to the pictures?

Nat
tin
tap
pin
pan

High-frequency Words
These high-frequency (common) words are in the story you have just read. Can you read them super fast?

is
it
a

Summary page to
reinforce learning

Practice of
high-frequency words

Phonics and Book Banding Consultant: Kate Ruttle

LADYBIRD BOOKS

UK | USA | Canada | Ireland | Australia
India | New Zealand | South Africa

Ladybird Books is part of the Penguin Random House group of companies
whose addresses can be found at global.penguinrandomhouse.com.

www.penguin.co.uk www.puffin.co.uk www.ladybird.co.uk

Penguin
Random House
UK

A version of this book was previously published as
Nat Naps! – Ladybird I'm Ready for Phonics: Level 2, 2014
This edition published 2018
001

Copyright © Ladybird Books Ltd, 2014, 2018

Printed in China

A CIP catalogue record for this book is available from the British Library

ISBN: 978-0-241-31254-4

All correspondence to
Ladybird Books
Penguin Random House Children's
80 Strand, London WC2R 0RL

It is Nat!

Written by Catherine Baker
Illustrated by Chris Jevons

Is it a pin?

It is Nat.

Is it a pan?

It is Nat.

Is it a tap?

10

It is Nat.

Is it a tin?

It is Nat.

It is Nat.

pan   pin   tin

14

tap

Nat

Story Words

Can you match these words to the pictures?

Nat

tin

tap

pin

pan

High-frequency Words

These high-frequency (common) words are in the story you have just read. Can you read them super fast?

is

it

a

Nat Sits

Written by Catherine Baker
Illustrated by Chris Jevons

It is Nat.

Nat sits.
Nat is in a pan.

Nat is in a tin.
Nat sits in it.

23

An ant.

A tin tips.

It is a tap.

27

Nat naps!

Story Words

Can you match these words to the pictures?

Nat

tip

tap

nap

ant